TRIC

LATERAL
THINKING
PUZZLES

Paul Sloane & Des MacHale

Illustrated by Myron Miller

Sterling Publishing Co., Inc.
New York

Edited by Peter Gordon

Library of Congress Cataloging-in-Publication Data

Sloane, Paul, 1950–
    Tricky lateral thinking puzzles / Paul Sloane & Des MacHale ;
illustrated by Myron Miller.
        p.   cm.
    Includes index.
    ISBN 0-8069-1248-0
    1. Lateral thinking puzzles.   I. MacHale, Des.   II. Title.
    III. Title: Lateral thinking puzzles.
    GV1507.L37S563   1999
    793.73—dc21   99–15855
                                                                        CIP

10 9 8 7 6 5 4

Published by Sterling Publishing Company, Inc.
387 Park Avenue South, New York, N.Y. 10016
© 1999 by Paul Sloane and Des MacHale
Distributed in Canada by Sterling Publishing
c/o Canadian Manda Group, One Atlantic Avenue, Suite 105
Toronto, Ontario, Canada M6K 3E7
Distributed in Great Britain and Europe by Cassell PLC
Wellington House, 125 Strand, London WC2R 0BB, England
Distributed in Australia by Capricorn Link (Australia) Pty Ltd.
P.O. Box 6651, Baulkham Hills, Business Centre, NSW 2153, Australia

Sterling ISBN 0-8069-1248-0

Acknowledgments

Thanks to Michael Humphrey for contributing "Sick Leave" and "Floating Home"; Richard Morton Jack for "The Wedding Present" and for help with editing; Micheal O'Fiachra for "Foreign Cure" and "Bus Lane Bonus"; John MacHale (age 11) for "Sign Here"; and Ann and Hannah Sloane for help with editing and for family support, which is always appreciated.

CONTENTS

INSTRUCTIONS

The puzzles in this book are all of a type known as lateral thinking puzzles, or situation puzzles. They should be fun—but they also help to develop skills in questioning, deduction, logic, and lateral thinking. They are based on a statement of a situation that you have to use as a starting point in order to arrive at a particular explanation or solution. Often there can be many possible scenarios that explain the puzzle, but you have to find the "right" answer.

It is better to do these puzzles in a small group rather than trying to solve them individually. Typically they contain insufficient information for you to immediately deduce the solution. You need to ask questions in order to gather more information before you can formulate solutions.

One person acts as quizmaster. He or she reads the puzzle aloud and reads the solution silently. The others ask questions in order to gather information, check assumptions, and test possible solutions. The quizmaster can answer in one of four ways: "Yes," "No," "Irrelevant," or "Please rephrase the question."

If people get stuck, the quizmaster can offer one or more of the clues given in the Clues section. The aim is to arrive at the solution given in the Answers section, not simply to find a situation that satisfies the initial conditions.

As with most problems we face, it is best to start by testing your assumptions, and by asking broad questions that establish general conditions, motives, and actions. Don't narrow in on specific solutions until you have first established the broad parameters of what is going on.

When you get stuck, attack the problem from a new direction—think laterally!

THE PUZZLES

Tricky Puzzles

The Tracks of My Tires

The police found a murder victim and they noticed a pair of tire tracks leading to and from the body. They followed the tracks to a nearby farmhouse where two men and a woman were sitting on the porch. There was no car at the farmhouse and none of the three could drive. The police arrested the woman. Why?

Clues: 69/Answer: 88.

The Upset Woman

When the woman saw him she was upset. Even though she had never seen him before, she had left some food for him because she knew he would be hungry. But he could not reach the food because he had an iron bar across his back. He died soon after and the woman was pleased. What's going on?

Clues: 70–71/Answer: 89.

Bertha's Travels

Every day Bertha travels 30 miles in the course of her work. She doesn't travel in a wheeled vehicle and never has problems with traffic, the police, weather, or airports. What does she do?

Clues: 51/Answer: 74.

Sick Leave

Walter spent three days in the hospital. He was neither sick nor injured, but when it was time to leave he had to be carried out. Why?

Clues: 66/Answer: 85.

Top at Last

William was the least intelligent and laziest boy in a class of 30 students who took an examination. Yet when the results were announced, William's name was at the top of the list. How come?

Clues: 69/Answer: 87.

Criminal Assistance

The police put up notices warning the public about a certain type of crime, but this actually helped the criminals. How?

Clues: 53/Answer: 76.

In the Middle of the Night

A man wakes up at night in the pitch dark. He knows that on his bedside table are a razor, a watch, and a glass of water. How can he reach out onto the table and be sure to pick up the watch without touching either the razor or the glass of water?

Clues: 58/Answer: 79.

Honorable Intent

Six people who do not know each other get together to honor a seventh person unknown to all of them. Why?

Clues: 58/Answer: 79.

Shell Shock

Why do players very rarely win at the "shell game," where they have to say which of three shuffled shells covers a pea?

Clues: 65/Answer: 85.

Wonderful Weather

A ship sank in perfect weather conditions. If the weather had been worse, the ship would probably not have sunk. What happened?

Clues: 72/Answer: 90.

Material Witness

In the fabric shop, the curtains are neatly arranged by style. The floral-patterned ones are in a section marked "Floral," the plain ones are in a section marked "Plain," and the striped ones are in a section marked "Striped." But one pair with vertical blue stripes is not in the "Striped" section. Why not?

Clue: 61/Answer: 82.

Denise and Harry

Denise died at sea while Harry died on land. People were pleased that Harry had died and even more pleased that Denise had died. Why?

Clues: 54/Answer: 76.

Mechanical Advantage

A driver had a problem with his car in a remote area miles from the nearest garage. He stopped at a little candy store, where his problem was quickly solved. How?

Clues: 61/Answer: 82.

Lifesaver

A politician made a speech that saved his life even before he gave the speech. How?

Clues: 60/Answer: 81.

Unfinished Business

What work can a sculptor never finish?

Clues: 70/Answer: 88.

The Deadly Dresser

A healthy man got dressed and then lay down and died. Why?

Clues: 53/Answer: 76.

Landlubber

A man sailed single-handed around the world in a small boat. Yet he was always in sight of land. How come?

Clues: 59/Answer: 81.

Another Landlubber

A man went around the world in a ship. Yet he was always in sight of land. How come?

Clues: 51/Answer: 74.

Plane and Simple

A boy who is three feet tall puts a nail into a tree at his exact height. He returns two years later when he has grown by six inches and the tree has grown by twelve inches. How much taller is the nail than the boy?

Clues: 63/Answer: 83.

Jericho

A man was building a house when it collapsed all around him. He wasn't injured or upset, and he calmly started to rebuild it. What was going on?

Clues: 59/Answer: 80.

Superior Knowledge

When the mother superior returned to the convent after a weekend away, she immediately noticed that a man had been there—and that was strictly against the rules. How did she know?

Clues: 68/Answer: 87.

Half for Me and Half for You

It is said that Lucrezia Borgia once split an apple in half and shared it with a companion. Within 10 minutes her companion was dead and Lucrezia survived. How come?

Clues: 57/Answer: 78.

Rush Job

In 1849, a man went to the California gold rush hoping to make his fortune by selling tents to the miners. However, the weather was fine and the miners slept out in the open, so the man could sell no tents. But he made his fortune anyway and his name is famous to this day. How did he become rich and who is he?

Clues: 65/Answer: 85.

The Engraving

A woman saw an advertisement for a color engraving of Queen Elizabeth II for $1 and bought it. When it arrived, she had no cause for complaint, but she wasn't pleased. Why?

Clues: 55/Answer: 77.

Who Did It?

A child at school printed something rude on the wall and nobody owned up to doing it. How did the teacher find out who did it?

Clues: 71/Answer: 89.

Lethal Relief

A famine-stricken Third World country was receiving food aid from the West, but this inadvertently led to the deaths of several people. How?

Clues: 60/Answer: 81.

Hot Job

A man held up a bank on a hot day. He was caught later by the police. On a colder day he would probably not have been caught. Why?

Clues: 58/Answer: 79.

Chop Chop

Why was an ancient, rare, and healthy tree that stood well away from all buildings in the grounds of Cork University condemned to be cut down?

Clues: 52/Answer: 75.

Resistance

During the German advance and occupation of France in World War II, how did some French resistance fighters booby-trap rooms in a way that put Germans more at risk than French people?

Clues: 64/Answer: 84.

Basket Case

She was responsible for the deaths of many people, yet she was never charged. How come?

Clues: 51/Answer: 74.

Invisible Earnings

Nauru, in the South Pacific, has a high income per capita. But its wealth doesn't come from anything it grows, makes, or mines. Where does its wealth come from?

Clues: 58/Answer: 80.

Absolute Madness

Why were 20 sane people put into a mental hospital?

Clues: 51/Answer: 74.

WALLY Test I

From the World Association of Learning, Laughter, and Youth (WALLY) comes the WALLY Test! It is a set of quick-fire questions. They may look easy, but be warned—they are designed to trick you. Write down your answers on a piece of paper and then see how many you got right. The time limit is three minutes.

1. If a man bets you that he can bite his eye, should you take the bet?
2. If he now bets you that he can bite his other eye, should you take that bet?
3. How can you stand behind someone while he or she stands behind you?
4. What looks like a horse, moves likes a horse, and is as big as a horse but weighs nothing?
5. Who is bigger: Mr. Bigger or Mr. Bigger's son?
6. Tom's mother had three children. One was named April. One was named May. What was the third one named?
7. Where could you go to see an ancient pyramid, an iceberg, and a huge waterfall?
8. What has four fingers and a thumb but isn't a hand?
9. What multiplies by division?
10. What's white when it's dirty and black when it's clean?

Answers on page 91.

Terribly Tricky Puzzles

Spies Are Us

During World War I, two German spies often ate at the same restaurant, but they never sat together. How did they pass information?

Clues: 67/Answer: 86.

Tittle Tattle

You have seen many tittles in the last few minutes. What are they?

Clues: 69/Answer: 87.

Outstanding

What feature of *The Old Farmer's Almanac* made it vastly more popular than all its rivals for over 100 years in the rural U.S.?

Clues: 63/Answer: 83.

The Stuffed Cloud

A meteorologist was replaced in his job because of a stuffed cloud. What's a stuffed cloud?

Clues: 68/Answer: 87.

A Strange Collection

At a dinner, a small container is passed around the table and every guest puts something in it. The contents are then thrown away. What's going on?

Clues: 67/Answer: 87.

Foreign Cure

Why does an American fly to another country in the hope of finding a cure for his illness?

Clues: 56/Answer: 77.

Bus Lane Bonus

A city introduced bus lanes on busy streets and the death rate dropped quickly. Why?

Clues: 52/Answer: 74.

Blow by Blow

Why was a man at a fairground blowing darts through a concealed blowpipe?

Clues: 51/Answer: 74.

History Question

What happened in London on September 8, 1752?

Clues: 57/Answer: 79.

Sign Here

A man bought two identical signs but found that he could use only one of them. Why?

Clues: 66/Answer: 86.

Paper Tiger

A man writes the same number, and nothing else, on 20 sheets of paper. Why?

Clues: 63/Answer: 83.

Forging Ahead

A forger went into a store with a genuine $50 bill. How did he use this to come out with a $20 profit?

Clues: 56/Answer: 77–78.

Smile Please!

A man wrote to a toothpaste company suggesting a way in which they could significantly increase their sales. How?

Clues: 67/Answer: 86.

High on a Hill

A man was marooned overnight on a mountain above the snow line in winter. He had no protective clothing and no tent. How did he survive?

Clues: 57/Answer: 79.

Mine Shafted

In order to sell it, a con man salted a useless mine with a number of genuine pieces of silver. How did the buyer figure out the scheme?

Clues: 61/Answer: 82.

That Will Teach You

One day a man came home to collect something he had forgotten, and found that his house had been completely destroyed. What had happened?

Clues: 68/Answer: 87.

A Geography Question

Which states of the U.S. are the most western, most southern, most northern, and most eastern?

Clues: 57/Answer: 78.

The Generous General

A retired English general was saddened to see a beggar on the street with a sign reading "World War II veteran." So he gave him £10. The man thanked him and the general became angry. Why?

Clues: 56/Answer: 78.

Fast Mover!

How did a man with an out-of-date passport legitimately visit 30 different countries in the same day?

Clues: 55/Answer: 77.

Running on Empty

Mrs. Jones was very pleased that the car ran out of gas. Why?

Clues: 64/Answer: 85.

What's the Point?

Why does a woman always use a square pencil in the course of her work?

Clues: 71/Answer: 89.

The Office Job

A man applied for a job in an office. When he arrived at the busy, noisy office he was told by the receptionist to fill out a form and then wait until called. He completed the form and then sat and waited along with four other candidates who had arrived earlier. After a few minutes, he got up and went into an inner office and was subsequently given the job. The other candidates who had arrived earlier were angry. The manager explained why the man had been given the job. What was the reason?

Clues: 62/Answer: 83.

Hearty Appetite

A whale ate normally and many people were very disappointed. Why?

Clues: 57/Answer: 79.

The Upset Bird Watcher

A keen ornithologist saw a rare bird that he had never seen before, except in illustrations. However, he was very upset. Then he was frightened. Why?

Clues: 70/Answer: 89.

Floating Home

A man went on a long trip and was gone several weeks. When he returned, he was found floating at sea. How come?

Clues: 55/Answer: 77.

Co-lateral Damage

During World War II, U.S. forces lost many bombers in raids over Germany due to antiaircraft fire. From the damage on returning bombers, they were able to build up a clear picture of which parts of the planes were hit most frequently and which weren't hit at all. How did they use this information to reduce losses?

Clues: 52/Answer: 75.

Orson Cart

When Orson Welles caused nationwide panic with his radio broadcast of the Martian landing, there was one group that wasn't fooled. Who were they?

Clues: 62/Answer: 83.

Throwing His Weight About

Why did a man who was not suicidal and not threatened in any way throw himself through a plate-glass window on the 24th floor of an office building and so fall to his death?

Clues: 68/Answer: 87.

Disconnected?

A horse walked all day. Two of its legs traveled 21 miles and two legs traveled 20 miles. How come?

Clues: 54/Answer: 77.

Joker

Four people were playing cards. One played a card and another player immediately jumped up and started to take her clothes off. Why?

Clues: 59/Answer: 80.

Rich Man, Poor Man

In England, why did rich people pour their tea first and then add milk while poor people poured milk first and then added tea?

Clues: 64/Answer: 84.

Mined Over Matter

A sailor at the bow of his ship saw a mine floating in the water directly in the path of the vessel. There was no time to change the ship's direction. How did he avert disaster?

Clues: 61/Answer: 82.

Surprise Visit

A factory manager gets a tip that the company chairman is on his way to pay a surprise visit. The manager orders the staff to clean the factory, clear out all the trash, and hide it away, but the chairman wasn't impressed. Why not?

Clues: 68/Answer: 87.

School's Out

Why does an elderly lady receive a court order to go to school immediately?

Clues: 65/Answer: 85.

The Deadly Stone

A man shot himself because he saw a stone with a small drop of blood on it. Why?

Clues: 54/Answer: 76.

The Costly Wave

A man waved his hands in the air and this action cost him $30,000. Why?

Clues: 53/Answer: 75.

WALLY Test II

Time for another WALLY Test. The questions may look easy, but be warned—they're designed to trip you up. Write down your answers on a piece of paper and then see how many you got right. The time limit is three minutes.

1. What gets higher as it falls?
2. How do you stop moles from digging in your garden?
3. Why did the overweight actor fall through the theater floor?
4. What happened to the man who invented the silent alarm clock?
5. What's the best known star with a tail?
6. How did an actor get his name up in lights in every theater in the country?
7. Where would you find a square ring?
8. What do you give a bald rabbit?
9. How do you make a slow horse fast?
10. Why did Sam wear a pair of pants with three large holes?

Answers on page 92.

Tremendously Tricky Puzzles

2020 Vision

A newspaper editor heard a report that 2020 pigs had been stolen from a farm, so he called the farmer to check the story. The farmer told him the same story, but the editor changed the number for insertion in the news. Why?

Clues: 69/Answer: 88.

The Deadly Omelet

A man went into a country inn and ordered an omelet for lunch. He was promptly arrested and later executed. Why?

Clues: 53/Answer: 76.

The Gap

A man was writing the word HIM. Why did he deliberately leave a gap between the final two letters so that it looked a little like HI M?

Clues: 56/Answer: 78.

The Dinner Clue

A suspect is interrogated for several hours but doesn't crack. He then demands a meal and soon afterward the police charge him with murder. Why?

Clues: 54/Answer: 76.

Wrong Way

Why does a man who wants to catch a bus going from Alewife to Zebedee deliberately catch one going the opposite way—from Zebedee to Alewife?

Clues: 72/Answer: 90.

The Single Word

A woman whom I had never met before was introduced to me. I didn't say a word. She told me about herself, but I didn't say a word. She told me many more things about herself, but I didn't say a word. Eventually I said one word and she was very disappointed. What was the word?

Clues: 66/Answer: 86.

The Man Who Would Not Read

A tourist in England was traveling by train. He had a book with him that he wanted to read, but he didn't start it until he got off the train. Why?

Clues: 60/Answer: 81.

Not Eating?

A hungry man has food on his plate but doesn't eat it. Why?

Clues: 62/Answer: 82.

Two Pigs

A farmer has two pigs that are identical twins from the same litter. However, when he sells them he gets 100 times more for one than the other. Why?

Clues: 70/Answer: 88.

Eensy Weensy Spider Farm

In some parts of France there are spider farms. Why would anybody want to farm spiders?

Clues: 55/Answer: 77.

Face-off

In World War I, the French and Austrian armies faced each other. Neither side attacked the other nor fired a shot at the other, yet thousands were killed. How?

Clues: 55/Answer: 77.

Cheap and Cheerful

A man at a party is offered a choice of a certain food—either the expensive fresh variety or the cheaper canned variety. Why does he choose the cheaper canned food?

Clues: 52/Answer: 74.

Up in Smoke

A man owned some excellent cigars, which he smoked. As a result of this he gained $10,000 and a prison sentence. How?

Clues: 70/Answer: 88.

Silly Cone

How did an office manager achieve greater efficiency using cones?

Clues: 66/Answer: 86.

Not the Führer

A body that looked very like that of Adolf Hitler was found by advancing Allied troops near Hitler's bunker in Berlin. The face was destroyed. How did the soldiers quickly find out that it wasn't Hitler's body?

Clues: 62/Answer: 83.

Vase and Means

∙∙∙

How did the ancient potters discover the ingredient that made perfect china?

Clues: 71/Answer: 89.

My Condiments to the Chef

∙∙∙

Why did the owner of a café replace all the bottles of condiments on his tables with packets?

Clues: 62/Answer: 82.

The Man Who Did Not Fly

∙∙∙

Why was a fictitious name added to an airline's passenger list?

Clues: 60/Answer: 81.

Inheritance

∙∙∙

In ancient Ireland, a king had two sons, each of whom wanted to inherit the kingdom. The king decreed that each should be put in a separate rowboat about one mile from shore and told to row in. The first to touch the shore would inherit the kingdom. The elder and stronger son rowed more quickly and was about to touch the shore with the younger son some 20 yards behind him and farther out to sea. How did the younger son inherit the kingdom?

Clues: 58/Answer: 79.

Stamp Dearth Death

A man died because he didn't buy enough stamps. What happened?

Clues: 67/Answer: 86.

Rock of Ages

A man suffered a serious injury because he was listening to rock-and-roll music. What happened?

Clues: 64/Answer: 84.

Quo Vadis?

How was an archaeologist in Britain able to deduce that the Romans drove their chariots on the left-hand side of the road?

Clues: 64/Answer: 84.

Pork Puzzler

Why did a man who didn't like bacon always pack some bacon when he went on a trip, and throw it out when he arrived?

Clues: 63/Answer: 83.

Frozen Assets

Why did they build a railway line over the ice when the place could be reached by land and they knew the ice would melt anyway?

Clues: 56/Answer: 78.

Turned Off

A man inadvertently caused all radio station transmissions in the world to cease. How? And who was he?

Clues: 69/Answer: 88.

The Last Mail

A man mailed two letters to the same address at the same time in the same post office. The letters were identical but the postage on one letter was more than on the other. Why?

Clues: 59–60/Answer: 81.

Small Is Not Beautiful

Why were small cars banned in Sweden?

Clues: 66–67/Answer: 86.

The Deadly Feather

A man lies dead next to a feather that caused his death. What happened?

Clues: 53/Answer: 76.

The Sealed Room

A perfectly healthy man was trapped in a sealed room. He died, but not from lack of oxygen. What did he die of?

Clues: 65/Answer: 85.

Written Down

A woman is writing in capital letters. She has difficulty writing the letters A, E, F, G, H, and L, but no difficulty with C, K, M, N, V, and W. Why?

Clues: 72/Answer: 90.

Publicity Puzzler

A man put an ad in the newspaper. As a result of this, he and another man go shopping together twice a year, but have no other contact. Why?

Clues: 63/Answer: 84.

Who Wants It Anyway?

He who has it is worried. He who loses it is poorer. He who wins it no longer has it. What is it?

Clue: 72/Answer: 90.

Knights of Old

What action carried out by knights because of their armor has persisted to this day, when no one wears armor?

Clues: 59/Answer: 80.

Shave That Pig!

"Barber, Barber, shave a pig" goes an old nursery rhyme. Why would anyone want to shave a live pig?

Clues: 65/Answer: 85.

Watch Out!

A man left his house to get a drink but died because his watch stopped. Why?

Clues: 71/Answer: 89.

The Wedding Present

A man bought a beautiful and appropriate wedding gift for a friend's wedding. The gift was wrapped and sent. When the gift was opened at the wedding, the man was highly embarrassed. Why?

Clues: 71/Answer: 89.

Murder Mystery

A woman murders her husband. She gains no advantage for herself in doing so. The police knew she did it. She was never charged with murder. What was going on?

Clues: 61/Answer: 82.

THE CLUES

Absolute Madness

They were received into the hospital as insane.

They had not carried out any action to indicate that they were insane.

They hadn't met before, but there was a link between them.

They had all set out to travel by bus.

Another Landlubber

He went around quite quickly.

He saw Africa, Asia, Europe, North America, and South America.

He didn't sail the ship.

Basket Case

She was very well known in her time.

She was involved in the execution of people.

She never said a word.

Bertha's Travels

Bertha is a woman who normally travels with other people.

She doesn't travel by walking or running, nor by plane or boat.

She provides a service to passengers.

Blow by Blow

He was secretly blowing darts at particular targets.

His nefarious actions generated more sales at the fairground.

Bus Lane Bonus

The bus lanes were introduced because of heavy traffic congestion. Normal traffic was forbidden to use the bus lanes so the buses could move more quickly.

The reduction in death rate wasn't due to fewer road accidents, fewer pedestrian accidents, less pollution, or fewer cars in the city.

Accident victims were saved.

Cheap and Cheerful

The fresh food was in perfectly good condition.

The man was normal and didn't have any allergies or aversions.

The food was salmon.

Chop Chop

The tree was not hazardous, harmful, or threatening in any way.

The problem does not involve animals, students, seeds, leaves, roots, or branches.

The problem related to the tree's location.

Co-lateral Damage

Some damage is fatal to a plane and some is not.

The returning planes are not a true sample of all the planes and all the damage.

U.S. bomber command used the information about damage on returning planes to strengthen planes and so reduce losses.

The Costly Wave

He wasn't at an auction.

He waved to fans and onlookers.

Criminal Assistance

The police notices were to warn people about certain types of thieves.

The thieves observed people's reactions to the signs.

The Deadly Dresser

If he had not dressed, he would not have died.

He died by accident.

He was poisoned.

The Deadly Feather

The man was physically fit and healthy.

The feather had touched him.

He was a circus performer.

The Deadly Omelet

He was a wanted man.

The omelet and its ingredients were relevant.

He had not done anything illegal.

This incident happened in France.

The Deadly Stone

The blood on the stone was the man's blood. It had been put there two days before his death.

Nobody else was involved.

He had marked the stone with his blood for a purpose.

Denise and Harry

Denise and Harry harmed people.

They weren't humans but they weren't animals either.

The Dinner Clue

The police obtained the evidence they needed.

He didn't finish his meal.

Disconnected?

The horse was alive throughout and was not exceptional.

The horse was a working horse.

The two legs that traveled farthest were the front left and back left.

WHAT THE HECK HAVE YOU BEEN DOING?

Eensy Weensy Spider Farm

It was relevant that the spider farms were in France.

The spiderwebs were used, but not to catch anything.

They are found in wine-growing regions.

The Engraving

What she received wasn't what she expected.

A fine artist had created the picture she received.

The engraving had already been put to use.

Face-off

The soldiers were killed, but not in action, nor by disease, flood, storm, or fire.

It was during winter.

Some test shots were fired, but the shells fell well away from the soldiers.

Fast Mover!

The man didn't use airplanes or super-fast ground transport.

He did not need his passport.

Floating Home

The man was normal, but he had been on an extraordinary voyage.

He had not set off by sea, but he had always intended to return in the manner in which he did.

He returned safe and well. He was found by people who were concerned for his well-being.

Foreign Cure

He didn't go abroad for drugs, medicines, treatments, or cures that were unavailable in the U.S.

His illness was curable given the right motivation.

He went to an Arab country.

Forging Ahead

He used the $50 bill to help pass a forged bill—but not a forged $50 bill.

He bought something he didn't want.

Frozen Assets

The railway was needed temporarily to carry cargo to a certain location.

It was possible to lay tracks over the land to reach the place, but they were unable to do so.

They wanted to supply food and ammunition.

The Gap

He was writing in an unusual way.

The writing was important and would be seen by many people.

He was planning ahead.

The Generous General

The general felt he had been misled.

The recipient's response wasn't what the general expected.

A Geography Question

Three of the answers are routine, but one is unexpected—and lateral!

Maine isn't the most eastern state.

Half for Me and Half for You

Lucrezia Borgia's companion died of poisoning.

The apple was taken at random from a bowl of perfectly good apples.

Lucrezia deliberately killed her companion.

Hearty Appetite

The whale was a killer whale.

The whale was at sea.

The people who were disappointed hadn't come to see the whale.

High on a Hill

The man managed to stay warm but he didn't burn anything.

The man was alone. No person or animal helped him to keep warm.

The mountain was dangerous.

History Question

September 8, 1752, was a very unusual day—but there were 10 other days like it.

No significant wars, births, deaths, disasters, achievements, or discoveries happened in London that day.

Honorable Intent

The six people had never met the seventh person and never would meet him.

The seventh person wasn't famous, remarkable, or well known.

The six people all owed a great debt to the seventh person—but not a financial debt.

Hot Job

The robber's face was covered, but he was easily identified.

His choice of clothing was poor.

Inheritance

Both sons reached the shore. The younger was judged to have touched the shore first.

The younger son took drastic action.

In the Middle of the Night

He didn't hear or smell anything that might have helped him.

The watch wasn't luminous.

None of the objects could be seen in the pitch dark.

Invisible Earnings

Nauru exports something of value.

It has nothing to do with tourism, finance, or crafts.

There are many seabirds in Nauru.

Jericho

Although he constructed it with great care, the man thought that the house might fall down.

He didn't intend that he or anyone else live in the house.

Joker

They weren't playing strip poker and stripping wasn't a forfeit or penalty involved in the game.

The actual card game isn't relevant.

She took off her clothes to avoid harm.

Knights of Old

It doesn't concern horses or weapons.

The custom has evolved and is used today by military personnel for a different purpose.

Originally it involved sight and recognition.

Landlubber

He circumnavigated the world and crossed every line of longitude.

There was nothing special about his boat or on his boat.

He sailed his boat around the world but always stayed within a few miles of shore.

He did it from November to February.

The Last Mail

There was no difference in the contents, envelope, or addressing of the two letters.

They were both sent by the same method—first class.

The same clerk at the same post office handled both letters.

The man weighed the letters and found their weights were identical. He then put stamps on them and took them to the postal clerk, who told him that one of the letters was fine but that the other needed more stamps.

Lethal Relief

They didn't die of hunger, disease, or food poisoning.

The relief was delivered to remote areas.

The people died before they opened the packages of food.

Lifesaver

Any speech of the same length would have had the same effect.

Someone made an attempt on his life.

The Man Who Did Not Fly

The fictitious person did not exist and did not fly.

The police knew about this situation.

Other passengers had been victims of a crime.

The Man Who Would Not Read

Conditions on the train were perfectly suitable for reading.

He was very obedient.

No local resident would have made the same mistake.

Material Witness

They are perfectly normal curtains and not special.

Mechanical Advantage

The problem wasn't with the engine of his car.

It was raining.

He bought something sweet and used that to solve the problem.

Mined Over Matter

The mine was live and dangerous. It would explode if it came into contact with metal.

He took some action to deflect the mine from the ship.

He did not touch or defuse the mine.

Mine Shafted

The buyer explored the mine and found the silver as was intended.

They were genuine pieces of silver but not the sort you would find in a silver mine.

Murder Mystery

Both the husband and wife had been married before.

Their marriage was successful and neither was unfaithful to the other.

She killed her husband to help someone she loved.

My Condiments to the Chef

The owner wasn't trying to save money or be more efficient.

There had been a problem involving the bottles of vinegar.

He was trying to discourage a certain group of customers.

Not Eating?

The hungry man wanted to eat and there was no medical, religious, or financial reason for him not to eat.

He was physically fit, healthy, and normal.

He was in the same room as his plate and the plate had food on it. But he wasn't able to eat it.

Not the Führer

There was no identity tag or personal effects that would have revealed the man's identity.

There were no distinguishing marks on the man's body.

His clothing gave the clue.

The Office Job

The man's age, appearance, gender, and dress didn't matter.

Everyone had completed the form correctly and in a similar fashion.

The man showed that he had a skill required for the job.

Orson Cart

The group that wasn't fooled did not know the plot of the play or the book, nor did they spot any production flaw.

They were children.

Outstanding

The feature of *The Old Farmer's Almanac* that made it more popular had nothing to do with its printed contents.

It had no value other than as an almanac.

Its advantage was practical.

Paper Tiger

The sheets of paper were important. He wrote the numbers in ink.

He intended to keep the papers for his later personal use.

He did this each year at a certain time of year.

Plane and Simple

The tree was normal and the boy was normal.

Trees grow differently from boys.

Pork Puzzler

The bacon served a purpose on the journey but was never used as food.

He packed it at the top of his suitcase.

Bacon is offensive to certain people.

Publicity Puzzler

The two men both share a problem. It's an unusual problem. It's not identical for each man.

By shopping together they gain a financial benefit.

They shop for one type of item only. It's not food, furniture, or electrical goods.

Quo Vadis?

The archaeologist didn't use any written or pictorial evidence.

He deduced that Romans drove their chariots on the left-hand side of the road from physical evidence. But not from the remains of chariots.

He excavated a Roman quarry.

Resistance

The booby traps depended on a likely action that Germans might take.

Germans have a reputation for being well organized, neat, and tidy.

Rich Man, Poor Man

It has nothing to do with the costs or prices of tea or milk.

It has nothing to do with the taste or flavor of the tea.

It concerns the cups from which they drank their tea.

Rock of Ages

He was oblivious to all around him.

He was struck with a strong blow.

His wife tried to help him.

Running on Empty

Something bad was averted.

Nobody was driving the car when it ran out of gas.

Rush Job

He exploited a different need of the miners.

He turned the tents to some other use—not accommodation.

The tents were made of heavy denim material.

School's Out

She was instructed to go to school for her education.

She was already very old (and well educated).

She was issued the court order automatically.

The Sealed Room

Nothing else and nobody else was involved except the man and the sealed room.

He died slowly but not from lack of food, water, or oxygen. If he had not been in the sealed room, he would have lived.

Shave That Pig!

The pigs were used for something other than food.

This happened only in winter.

Shell Shock

The game is rigged.

The dealer is fast, but it isn't speed alone that deceives the player.

Sick Leave

Walter was human and physically normal.

The hospital was a normal hospital.

He wasn't able to walk into the hospital or out of it.

Sign Here

He had intended to use the two signs in two places to give the same message, but he found that that didn't work.

He was advertising his roadside café.

Silly Cone

The office manager found a way to make people waste less time.

The cones were given away free.

A cone will not rest on its end.

The Single Word

Other people also heard what she had to say.

There is no sexual connotation to this story. The narrator could be male or female.

The word I said summarized a decision that would significantly affect the woman.

None of my companions was allowed to speak in the woman's presence.

Small Is Not Beautiful

It doesn't have to do with pollution, crime, economy, car production, or politics.

The reason concerned safety.

Small cars were more dangerous in certain types of accidents that occur often in Sweden.

Smile Please!

The toothpaste company adopted his idea and their sales increased.

It had nothing to do with the taste, price, or distribution of the toothpaste.

The idea encouraged people to use more toothpaste.

Spies Are Us

They went to the restaurant as paying customers.

No codes were used, and they never spoke or sat near each other.

They dressed in similar clothes.

Stamp Dearth Death

If he had bought the right postage, he would have lived.

He sent a package.

A Strange Collection

The contents are inedible, but they are not bones or animal parts.

They had done something relevant together earlier in the day.

They are eating game.

The Stuffed Cloud

The meteorologist died.

He wasn't aware of the stuffed cloud. It hadn't affected any of his forecasts or reports.

He was traveling.

Superior Knowledge

Nobody said anything, but there was visible evidence of the man's presence.

It was nothing to do with shaving.

Surprise Visit

The factory manager and his staff cleared away all the rubbish and left the factory looking spotlessly clean.

The chairman arrived in an unexpected fashion.

He saw a terrible mess.

That Will Teach You

This didn't happen at night.

He hadn't left any heating, lighting, or cooking equipment on.

The thing he had forgotten had helped cause a fire.

Throwing His Weight About

The man was normal, fit, and healthy.

He died by accident.

He was trying to demonstrate something.

Tittle Tattle

Tittles are seen in print.

There are two in this sentence.

Top at Last

William didn't cheat.

He didn't revise or work any harder than usual.

He wasn't particularly happy to be top of the list.

The Tracks of My Tires

The police didn't ask any questions but merely used their powers of observation.

When the police arrived, none of the three suspects was carrying a weapon or wearing blood-stained clothing.

The police correctly deduced that the woman was the murderer.

Turned Off

The man didn't interfere with the physical operation of the radio stations.

There was no threat or misinformation.

All radio stations voluntarily chose to stop transmitting for a short period.

2020 Vision

The farmer was being truthful.

Exactly 22 pigs were stolen.

Two Pigs

They were sold on the same day at the same market.

Each was sold for a fair price.

The two pigs looked the same, but when they were sold one was worth much more than the other.

One was sold for food—the other was not.

Unfinished Business

The work isn't necessarily big.

Many people undertake this work.

None of them can ever truly complete it.

Up in Smoke

The cigars were valuable. He didn't steal or sell them.

He was perfectly entitled to smoke them.

He successfully claimed the $10,000, and as a result was found guilty of a crime.

The Upset Bird Watcher

The bird was just as beautiful and rare as he had imagined. He wasn't disappointed with its appearance.

What happened to the bird placed him at risk.

He saw the bird through a small window.

The Upset Woman

He was an unwelcome intruder.

He had visited before, so she left some food for him.

She wanted him to die.

Vase and Means

They discovered the ingredient by accident.

The ingredient strengthened the pottery.

The accident was a tragedy.

Watch Out!

The man thought it was much later than it actually was.

It was dark when he went outside.

The man was unusual.

The Wedding Present

He was embarrassed with shame when his gift was opened.

His gift wasn't offensive to the bride and groom in any religious, political, or moral way.

He had bought an expensive gift but then made a mistake and tried to save money.

What's the Point?

A round pencil would not do.

She hates losing pencils.

Who Did It?

The teacher didn't threaten or bribe any child.

No child admitted the misdemeanor or tattled on anyone else.

The teacher gave the class an exercise to do.

Who Wants It Anyway?

It's something that can be won or lost. If you lose it, then you suffer financial and other penalties.

Wonderful Weather

The accident happened at night.

No other craft was involved.

The accident happened in winter.

Written Down

She is writing in an unusual place.

She has difficulty writing the letters P, R, T, and Z but no difficulty with O, Q, S, U, X, and Y.

She is writing on thick books.

Wrong Way

The man had a rational reason for choosing a bus going in the opposite direction to the one he wanted.

His reason was not to do with saving money, saving time, avoiding danger, seeing anything, or meeting anyone.

His reason has to do with comfort.

THE ANSWERS

Absolute Madness
A bus driver was told to bring 20 psychiatric patients to a mental hospital. On the way he stopped to buy a newspaper. When he got back, all his passengers had gone. So he drove up to several bus stops and collected the first 20 passengers he could find and delivered them to hospital, where he warned the staff that they would all cause trouble and claim to be sane.

Another Landlubber
He was an astronaut in a space ship.

Basket Case
She was "Madame Guillotine," the deadly invention of Joseph Guillotin that was used in France to execute people.

Bertha's Travels
Bertha is an elevator operator.

Blow by Blow
The assistant at the fairground blew darts through a concealed blowpipe to burst the balloons of children on their way home from the fair so that their parents would have to return to buy replacement balloons in order to stem the tears.

Bus Lane Bonus
Emergency vehicles and, in particular, ambulances were allowed to use the bus lanes. Ambulances reached accident victims sooner and got them to the hospital sooner so fewer of them died.

Cheap and Cheerful
The food is salmon. Previously he had choked on a bone in fresh salmon. The salt in canned salmon dissolves the bones and removes this danger.

Chop Chop
For a short time on sunny days, the shadow of the old tree covered an instrument used for recording sunshine. The instrument had been put in place on a cloudy day. Good sense prevailed and the instrument was moved instead.

Co-lateral Damage
They strengthened the parts of the aircraft that had not been hit. Antiaircraft fire is random in nature. The returning planes showed damage that had not been fatal. But this sample excludes information from the planes that had not returned and had sustained fatal damage. It was deduced that they had sustained damage on the parts not hit on the returning planes. By adding armor to the planes, overall losses were reduced.

The Costly Wave
The man was the winner of the prestigious London Marathon race. He waved to the large crowd the entire way down the finishing straightaway and, because of that, he just failed to break the record time for the marathon—thereby missing out on the $30,000 bonus prize.

Criminal Assistance

The police put up notices "Beware of Pickpockets." The pickpockets stood near a sign and noticed that when people saw it they immediately checked that their purses and wallets were safe. The pickpockets then knew where their victims carried their purses and wallets—which made them easier to steal.

The Deadly Dresser

The last thing he put on was his shoe and it contained a deadly spider that bit him, and he died soon after.

The Deadly Feather

The man was a circus sword swallower. In the middle of his act someone tickled him with the feather and he gagged.

The Deadly Omelet

The man was an aristocrat on the run from the French Revolution. He disguised himself as a peasant. When he ordered an omelet, he was asked how many eggs he wanted in it. He replied, "A dozen." No peasant would have asked for more than two or three.

The Deadly Stone

The man was lost in the desert. Without landmarks, he marked stones with a drop of blood from a cut on his hand. After two days of walking and out of water, he found a stone with blood on it. He knew that he was walking in circles and he shot himself rather than face a slower death.

Denise and Harry

Denise and Harry were hurricanes.

The Dinner Clue

The meal included a large piece of stale cheese that the suspect bit into and then left. His teeth marks were found to match a bite on the body of a murder victim.

Disconnected?
The horse worked in a mill. It walked around in a circle all day to drive the millstone. In the course of the day, its outer legs walked a mile farther than its inner legs.

Eensy Weensy Spider Farm
Spiderwebs are bought by unscrupulous wine merchants who want to give the impression that their wines are old and mature.

The Engraving
She received a used British postage stamp.

Face-off
The French tested their artillery by firing some shots into the mountains. This caused avalanches that killed many soldiers on both sides.

Fast Mover!
The man was a diplomatic courier and he visited the embassies of 30 countries, all situated in Washington. In law, an embassy is part of the country of the embassy and not part of the country in which it is situated.

Floating Home
The man was an astronaut.

Foreign Cure
The man is an alcoholic. He flies to a country where alcohol is banned by law in the hope of curing his addiction by removing the temptation.

Forging Ahead
The forger bought a cheap item with the genuine $50 bill. In the change he would usually get at least one $20 bill. He would then ask the storekeeper to change the $20 bill into two tens and switch the genuine $20 bill with a forged one

of his own making. The storekeeper was less likely to check a bill he believed he had just paid out.

Frozen Assets
During World War II, the Russians built a railway line over the frozen Lake Ladoga in order to deliver supplies to the city of Leningrad, which was under siege from German forces. Its population was starving and there was no means of supply from the Russian side other than over the lake.

The Gap
The man was carving a tombstone. A husband had died and the man carved
>   PRAY FOR
>   HI M.
When the wife died, she would be buried with her husband and the engraving would be amended to
>   PRAY FOR
>   THEM.

The Generous General
The soldier thanked him by saying, "*Danke schön*."

A Geography Question
Hawaii is the most southern and Alaska is simultaneously the most western, most northern, and most eastern. It's the most eastern because some remote islands that are part of Alaska lie over the 180-degree line of longitude and are therefore east of the continental U.S.

Half for Me and Half for You
Lucrezia Borgia put a deadly poison on one side of the blade of a knife. When she cut the apple, only one half was poisoned.

Hearty Appetite
After the *Exxon Valdez* oil spill, an enormous amount of money was spent cleansing the environment and rehabilitating oil-damaged animals. Two seals had been carefully nurtured back to good health at a cost of over $100,000, and they were released into the sea in front of an appreciative crowd. A few minutes later the crowd was horrified to see them both eaten by a killer whale.

High on a Hill
The man was marooned on a volcano that had recently erupted. He was kept alive by the heat of the melting lava.

History Question
Absolutely nothing happened in London on September 8, 1752. It was one of the eleven days dropped when the old calendar was adjusted to the new one.

Honorable Intent
The six people had all received different organs from a donor who had died in an accident. They meet to honor his memory.

Hot Job
The man wore a short-sleeved shirt and his name was tattooed on his arm.

Inheritance
The younger son took his sword and cut off his hand before hurling it ashore. Since he had touched the shore before his brother, he was able to claim his father's kingdom. (This story is told of the kingdom of Ulster, and to this day a bloody red hand is used as the symbol of the province.)

In the Middle of the Night
He turns on the light.

Invisible Earnings
Nauru exports guano, which is an excellent fertilizer. Guano comes from the droppings of seabirds.

Jericho
The man was building a house of cards.

Joker
When one player went to play a card, she knocked over a mug. The hot drink poured over the other player, who immediately jumped up and started to take her clothes off.

Knights of Old
When knights in full armor rode past the king, they would raise the visor on their helmet so that the king could see them. This action in turn became the salute that military personnel give to higher officers.

Landlubber
He sailed around the coast of Antarctica.

The Last Mail
Both letters were the same weight, a fraction under the weight at which a surcharge was charged. He put the correct postage amount in stamps on each letter. One had a single stamp of the correct value and the other had several stamps adding up to the correct value. When the letters were weighed, the one with the more stamps was over the limit and so more stamps were needed.

Lethal Relief
The food was dropped by parachute in remote areas. Several people were killed when the packages fell on them.

Lifesaver
The politician was Teddy Roosevelt, the American president. In 1912, in Milwaukee, he was shot in the chest. He was saved because the bullet was slowed as it passed through the folded manuscript of the speech in his breast pocket. He went on to make the speech later on the same day that he was shot!

The Man Who Did Not Fly
In this true case, many vacationers who flew with a certain airline had their homes burglarized while they were away. The police added a false name (but real address) to the list and caught the burglar red-handed when he broke in. It turned out that his sister worked for the airline and passed the list of passenger addresses to her nefarious brother.

The Man Who Would Not Read
He saw a notice on the side of the carriage that said, "This carriage is not for Reading." Reading is a town on the main line between London and Bristol.

Material Witness
They are on the window!

Mechanical Advantage
It was raining heavily and the man discovered a leak in the roof of his car. He bought several packs of chewing gum, chewed them, and then used the gum as a water-proof filler until he could reach a garage.

Mined Over Matter
The sailor used the water hose on the ship to direct a jet of water onto the mine to push it out of the path of the ship.

Mine Shafted
He had shredded real silver dollars to produce the silver. One piece was found with the word "unum" (from "e pluribus unum") on it.

Murder Mystery
The man and woman lie badly injured after a car accident. The wife knows that they are both going to die and she fears that she will die first. They recently married and have no children from this marriage but each has children from a previous marriage. If she dies first, then all of the joint estate will go to his children. She kills her husband so that her children will inherit the entire estate.

My Condiments to the Chef
Drug addicts were using his café and dipping their needles into his vinegar bottles because heroin is soluble in vinegar. He replaced the vinegar bottles with small packets of vinegar in order to stop the addicts from dipping their syringes into the bottles.

Not Eating?
His plate is his dental plate.

Not the Führer
When the shoes were removed from the body, the man was found to be wearing darned socks. The soldiers did not believe that the Führer of the Third Reich would wear darned socks.

The Office Job
This happened in the 1800s. The man had applied for a job as a telegraph operator. Among the background noise was a Morse code message saying, "If you understand this, walk into the office." It was a test of the candidates' skill and alertness. He was the only candidate who passed.

Orson Cart
Orson Welles's voice was recognized by the many children who listened to his regular children's radio show.

Outstanding
The Old Farmer's Almanac had a hole in the top left corner that made it ideal for hanging on a nail in the outhouse.

Paper Tiger
It's January and he is writing the date of the year on all the checks in his checkbook to avoid putting last year's date by mistake.

Plane and Simple
The boy will be six inches taller than the nail. The tree grows from the top, so the nail won't rise.

Pork Puzzler
The man was traveling to a strict Muslim country where alcohol was banned. He placed a small bottle of whiskey under a pack of bacon in his suitcase. He knew that if the customs officials at the airport of entry opened his suitcase they wouldn't touch the bacon and therefore his whiskey would be safe.

Publicity Puzzler
The man has feet of different sizes—his left foot is 12 and his right foot is 13. He advertises to find a man with the opposite—a left foot size 13 and right foot size 12. Together they go shopping to find a shoe style that suits them both. They then buy two pairs, one 12 and one 13, before swapping shoes.

Quo Vadis?
The archaeologist was excavating a Roman quarry. The ruts in the road leading from the quarry were much deeper on the left than on the right. Since the carts leaving the quarry were much heavier than those returning, he deduced that the Romans drove on the left side of the road.

Resistance
Pictures in buildings that would be occupied were hung at a slight angle and attached to bombs. The tidy Germans straightened the pictures with fatal results.

Rich Man, Poor Man
Rich people had bone china that could take the hot tea, but poor people had cheap crockery that would crack if hot tea were poured into it. Pouring the tea first became a sign of prosperity.

Rock of Ages
The man was listening to rock-and-roll music through his Walkman headphones in the kitchen. He had his hand on the kettle and his back to the door. When his wife came in, she saw him shaking violently but she heard no sound. She called to him but he didn't hear her. Thinking that he was suffering from an electric shock, she picked up a rolling pin and hit his arm, breaking it.

Running on Empty
Mr. and Mrs. Jones had had a silly argument. Mrs. Jones stormed out and the depressive Mr. Jones had tried to commit suicide by sitting in his car in the garage with the engine running. He passed out, but then the car ran out of gas and when Mrs. Jones returned she rescued him and they were reconciled.

Rush Job
He used the tough tent cloth to make trousers for the miners. His name was Levi Strauss.

School's Out
She has just celebrated her 105th birthday, but the computer at the local education authority cannot recognize a date of birth that is over 100 years ago. Calculating that she is 5 years old, the computer prints out an automatic instruction to attend school.

The Sealed Room
He died from carbon dioxide poisoning, which takes effect before oxygen starvation.

Shave That Pig!
In China, live pigs were used like hot-water bottles to keep people warm in bed on cold nights. For the sleepers' comfort, the pigs were shaved first.

Shell Shock
The pea isn't under any of the shells. It's slipped under a shell by the operator as he lifts it. Sometimes the operator places the pea under a player's choice to encourage dupes.

Sick Leave
Walter was a newborn baby.

Sign Here
He bought two identical signs for his café, but found that he needed two different ones for the two sets of traffic coming in different directions. The two signs said:
"FRED'S CAFÉ fi " and "< FRED'S CAFÉ"

Silly Cone
Drinking cups in the shapes of cones were provided at water fountains. Since they couldn't be put down, people had to quickly drink the water. This sped up their breaks.

The Single Word
The word was "Guilty." I was foreman of the jury at the woman's trial.

Small Is Not Beautiful
Small cars were banned in Sweden because of the high incidence of accidents involving collisions with moose. Occupants of small cars suffered serious injuries, but large cars offered more protection.

Smile Please!
The man suggested that they make the hole in the top of the tube bigger so that more toothpaste would be squeezed out each time.

Spies Are Us
The German spies wore identical hats with secret information hidden inside the hatband. They entered the restaurant at slightly different times and placed their hats on the hatrack where they could see them. They left at different times—each taking the other's hat.

Stamp Dearth Death
The man was a terrorist letter-bomber. He sent a letter bomb, but didn't put enough stamps on it. It was returned to him and it exploded, killing him.

A Strange Collection
The guests are eating pheasant, which they shot earlier that day. The container is for the pellets of lead shot.

The Stuffed Cloud
A stuffed cloud, in pilot slang, is a cloud with a mountain in it. The meteorologist was a passenger on a plane that hit a stuffed cloud. He was killed and had to be replaced at his job.

Superior Knowledge
One of the toilet seats had been left up.

Surprise Visit
The manager and staff dumped all the trash on the flat roof of the factory so that it wouldn't be seen. Unfortunately, the company chairman arrived by helicopter and landed on the roof.

That Will Teach You
The man left his glasses on his bedside table. They had focused the rays of the sun onto his pillow and started a fire that destroyed his house.

Throwing His Weight About
He was demonstrating how strong the glass was to a group of visitors. He threw himself against it, but it was not as strong as he had thought.

Tittle Tattle
A tittle is the dot on an i.

Top at Last
William's name was William Abbott, and the results were given in alphabetical order.

The Tracks of My Tires
The woman was the only person in a wheelchair.

Turned Off
The man was Guglielmo Marconi, the pioneer of radio transmission. When he died in 1937, all the radio stations in the world observed a minute of silence as a mark of respect.

2020 Vision
As he talked to the farmer on the phone, the newspaper editor realized that the man had a slight lisp and that what he had actually reported stolen was "two sows and twenty pigs."

Two Pigs
This happened in France. One pig was sold for bacon. The other had been painstakingly trained to sniff out truffles and was therefore very valuable.

Unfinished Business
His autobiography.

Up in Smoke
In this true story, the cigars were insured under the man's general household policy as named items. He claimed against his insurance company on the grounds that the cigars had been destroyed in a series of small fires. The insurance company rejected the claim, pointing out that he had started the fires in order to smoke the cigars. He took the insurance company to court and won the case. The judge ruled that the insurance policy covered against loss by fire and that this was what had happened. The man was awarded $10,000. However, as he left the court he was arrested by the police on a charge of arson, based on his sworn testimony. He was found guilty and given a one-year suspended prison sentence.

The Upset Bird Watcher
The ornithologist was sitting on a plane coming in to land when he saw the rare bird, which was sucked into the jet engine causing the engine to fail and the plane to crash-land.

The Upset Woman
He was a mouse caught in a mousetrap.

Vase and Means
Bone china was discovered when an unfortunate worker fell into the kiln and became part of the product. Animal bones are used nowadays.

Watch Out!
The man is Count Dracula, who leaves his house for his nightly drink of blood. However, his watch has stopped and what he thinks is night is actually a solar eclipse. He is caught in the sunlight and dies.

The Wedding Present
The man selected a beautiful crystal vase in a gift shop, but he knocked it over and broke it. He had to pay for it, so he instructed the shop to wrap it and send it anyway. He assumed that people would think that it had been broken in transit. Unfortunately for him, the shop assistant carefully wrapped every broken piece before sending the package.

What's the Point?
The woman is a carpenter who works on scaffolding at a building site. A conventional round pencil is more likely to roll off and fall.

Who Did It?
One of the words that was not rude was spelled incorrectly (for example, "The headmaster is a horribul %$@*&@!"). The teacher gave a spelling test that included the word and the guilty child spelled it wrong again.

Who Wants It Anyway?
A lawsuit.

Wonderful Weather
The ship was the *Titanic*, which hit an iceberg on a fine night when the sea was very flat. If the weather had been worse, then the lookouts would have seen waves hitting the iceberg or heard the iceberg. (Icebergs make groaning noises when they move.) Unfortunately the iceberg wasn't seen and the rest is history.

Written Down
She is writing along the top of a closed book—on the top of the pages. Any letter with a horizontal line in it is difficult, since the pen tends to slip down between the pages.

Wrong Way
The bus from Alewife to Zebedee is always full by the time it reaches the man's stop, so he catches one going the opposite way in order to get a seat on the bus for the return journey to Zebedee.

WALLY Test I Answers

Here are the answers to the first WALLY Test. Be prepared to groan!

1. No. He will take his glass eye out of its socket and bite it.
2. No. He will take out his false teeth and bite his good eye with them.
3. You stand back to back.
4. The shadow of a horse.
5. Mr. Bigger's son. No matter how big Mr. Bigger is, his son is a little Bigger!
6. Tom's mother's third child was named Tom.
7. Egypt, Greenland, and Niagara Falls.
8. A glove.
9. An amoeba.
10. A blackboard.

Rate your score on the following scale:

Number Correct	Rating
8 to 10	WALLY Whiz
6 to 7	Smart Aleck
3 to 5	WALLY
0 to 2	Ultra-WALLY

WALLY Test II Answers

More answers, more groans!

1. Snow.
2. Hide their shovels!
3. It was just a stage he was going through!
4. He was given the Nobel Prize.
5. Mickey Mouse.
6. He changed his name to Exit.
7. At a boxing arena.
8. A hare piece.
9. Don't feed him.
10. To get his feet in (all pants have three large holes).

Rate your score on the following scale:

Number Correct	Rating
8 to 10	WALLY Whiz
6 to 7	Smart Aleck
3 to 5	WALLY
0 to 2	Ultra-WALLY

About the Authors

PAUL SLOANE was born in Scotland and educated at Cambridge University, where he studied engineering. He has worked for many years in the computer industry, primarily in international software marketing. He has always been an avid collector and creator of lateral thinking puzzles. His first book, *Lateral Thinking Puzzlers*, was published by Sterling in 1991, and has gone on to become a bestseller. It has been translated into many languages. Following its success, he established himself as the leading expert in this kind of conundrum. He runs the lateral thinking puzzle forum on the Web at www.books.com and has his own home page. He is an acclaimed speaker on lateral thinking in business. He lives with his wife in Camberley, England, has three daughters, and tries to keep fit by playing chess, tennis, and golf.

DES MACHALE was born in County Mayo, Ireland, and is Associate Professor of Mathematics at University College in Cork. He and his wife, Anne, have five children. The author of over 40 books, including one on the John Ford cult film *The Quiet Man* and another on George Boole of Boolean algebra fame, Des MacHale has many interests. He has a large collection of crystals, minerals, rocks, and fossils; he was chairman of the International Conference on Humor in 1985; and his hobbies include broadcasting, film, photography, and numismatics. In fact, he is interested in just about everything except wine, jazz, and Demi Moore.

This is the seventh book coauthored by Paul Sloane and Des MacHale, following the success of their other lateral thinking puzzle books, also published by Sterling.

Index

Page key:
puzzle, *clues*, **answer**

Lateral Thinking Puzzle Books
by Paul Sloane and Des MacHale

Lateral Thinking Puzzlers
Paul Sloane, 1991
0-8069-8227-6

Challenging Lateral Thinking Puzzles
Paul Sloane & Des MacHale, 1993
0-8069-8671-9

Great Lateral Thinking Puzzles
Paul Sloane & Des MacHale, 1994
0-8069-0553-0

Test Your Lateral Thinking IQ
Paul Sloane, 1994
0-8069-0684-7

Improve Your Lateral Thinking: Puzzles to Challenge Your Mind
Paul Sloane & Des MacHale, 1995
0-8069-1374-6

Intriguing Lateral Thinking Puzzles
Paul Sloane & Des MacHale, 1996
0-8069-4252-5

Perplexing Lateral Thinking Puzzles
Paul Sloane & Des MacHale, 1997
0-8069-9769-2

Ingenious Lateral Thinking Puzzles
Paul Sloane & Des MacHale, 1998
0-8069-6259-3

Tricky Lateral Thinking Puzzles
Paul Sloane & Des MacHale, 1999
0-8069-1248-0

Ask for them wherever books are sold.